FINDING
YOUR OWN UNIVERSE

SIMPLE AND PRACTICAL ADVICE
ON HOW TO DISCOVER, NURTURE &
PRESERVE YOUR PERSONAL UNIVERSE

VISHAL V DHINGRA

INDIA · SINGAPORE · MALAYSIA

Notion Press

No.8, 3rd Cross Street,
CIT Colony, Mylapore,
Chennai, Tamil Nadu – 600004

First Published by Notion Press 2021
Copyright © Vishal V Dhingra 2021
All Rights Reserved.

ISBN 978-1-63781-425-3

This book has been published with all efforts taken to make the material error-free after the consent of the author. However, the author and the publisher do not assume and hereby disclaim any liability to any party for any loss, damage, or disruption caused by errors or omissions, whether such errors or omissions result from negligence, accident, or any other cause.

While every effort has been made to avoid any mistake or omission, this publication is being sold on the condition and understanding that neither the author nor the publishers or printers would be liable in any manner to any person by reason of any mistake or omission in this publication or for any action taken or omitted to be taken or advice rendered or accepted on the basis of this work. For any defect in printing or binding the publishers will be liable only to replace the defective copy by another copy of this work then available.

To my parents, who had no idea I was writing a book and were least bothered even after knowing that I wrote one.

Contents

Introduction   9

Part I

1. Your very own universe – wait, what?   15
2. What is your personal universe made of and how does it affect you?   18
   - The company we keep   18
   - Places we visit   20
   - Things we read   22
   - Things we watch   25
3. Gifts from the universe   28
   - The body   29
   - The brain   30
   - The comfort parody   32
   - Uniqueness   33
4. The powers of your universe   36
   - The power of thoughts   36
   - How do you know what you know?   36
   - The power of doing (karma)   39

The power of abundance		41
The power of reversal		43

Part II

5.	How to make your universe favourable	47
6.	Etiquette towards a favourable universe	50
	Don'ts for a favourable universe	50
	Don't overthink	51
	Don't fear	53
	STEP 1: What if I…	55
	STEP 2: What can I…	56
	STEP 3: How will I…	56
	Don't regret	58
	Don't compare or judge	58
7.	Challenges from your universe (after you have made it favourable)	60
	You will feel lost	61
	You will want to quit	62
	You will have to sacrifice a lot	62
	You will struggle with discipline	63
	You will feel lonely	64
	It will take longer than you expected	65
	There will be many, many distractions	66
	How to build focus	66
	Avoid multitasking	66
	Try meditation	67
	Develop a focusing habit	68

Part III

8.	Why are you still not getting what you asked for?	73
9.	Signals from your universe	75
	The lightning of joy	76
	Signals from your body	76
	Signals from your brain	77
10.	Questions we ask the universe (putting an end to existential crisis)	80
	Existential crisis	80
	What is the purpose of my life?	81
	Should we believe in luck or in hard work?	85
	The power of choice	90
	The 90/10 principle	92
	What is happiness (or how to be happy)?	94
	What is success?	96
	Myth: success is a general term	96
	Myth: it's easy once you get there	98
	Myth: they got lucky	99
	An ideal success mix	100
	Active Lifestyle vs Passive Lifestyle	101
	How to be successful?	104
	Visualisation	105
	Filtering out	106
	Treat everyone equally	107
	Be consistent	108
	Think of the greater good	108

Contents

How to stop being lazy and get going?	110
The motivation pyramid	114
There is a more traditional explanation of laziness.	116
A note from the author	*121*

Introduction

In these times, anyone can find information about anything with little effort. With just a click, you can learn the secrets of the galaxies or what your neighbour had for lunch. From simple facts to complex topics, everything can be found online. Just Google it!

Why, then, should you be reading this book? What does it offer that cannot be found online?

To begin with, this book will introduce you to something that has always existed around you (and that affects you deeply) but you have been unaware of its existence. Or, perhaps you know it's there but you have never paid it the attention it deserves.

This book will help you rediscover your very own personal universe and help you see the profound impact it has on your life.

In this process, you will address the problems that you know are there but often tend to overlook – problems that can't be solved by the internet.

What we believe in is what happens to us. Through this book, I have tried to highlight how our circumstances

Introduction

and our everyday actions affect us, and how we can harness our innate power to steer our life towards a more conscious, aware and evolved existence. Taking inspiration from the universe, I have citied many examples that will take you closer to the universe and the way it operates and, in turn, bring you closer to your own self.

The answers to so many of our problems are right in front of us, but a fast-paced life simply doesn't allow us to pause and look inwards. We are in a constant race to know it all, when, rather than just knowing, we need to focus on the source of our knowing. In other words, we need to think about these questions: How and why do I know what I know? Can I change what I know?

In this book, I have tried to offer answers to what people usually call the Existential Crisis. And worry not, for I have done it in the simplest way possible. Whenever in your life you are hit by an existential crisis, in this book you will find something to refer to, something that will help you sail through the situation.

In essence, this book seeks to answer many questions you may have asked yourself at some point – What is the purpose of my life? How can I be truly happy? What are feelings and who controls them? Should I believe in luck or hard work or luck? … and many more.

Chances are you might have looked for answers to these questions at least once in your lifetime, if not more. I did the same, and while looking for my answers

I realised that there is no article or book that gives these answers in a straight and simplified manner.

That's when I thought, why not write one myself?

Regardless of how old you are or at which stage of life, there will be at least one key learning that you can take away from this book and use it to live better.

I hope this is enough reason for you to read this book, or any self-help book for that matter.

I do urge you not to read the entire book in one go, as many of us tend to do. Because at times this book will challenge your current beliefs and gently nudge you to question them. Reading slowly will help you soak in the information and apply it your life, and also lead to a fulfilling reading experience, which is what I hope for every reader who picks up this book.

The book is divided into three parts, and each one aims to take you a step ahead and closer to your universe and its amazing secrets and principles.

Part I

1. Your very own universe – wait, what?
2. What is your personal universe made of and how does it affect you?
3. Gifts from the universe
4. Powers of your universe

Part II

5. How to make your universe favourable
6. Etiquette towards a favourable universe
7. Challenges from your universe (after you have made it favourable)

Part III

8. Why are you still not getting what you asked for?
9. Signals from your universe
10. Questions we ask the universe (putting an end to existential crisis)

Part I

Once, in an interview for admission in MBA, the interviewer asked me a wide range of questions, from photosynthesis to names of the parents of Mahatma Gandhi. It was a tough interview, but it went well.

When the interview was about to finish, the gentleman said to me, 'You are intelligent, but I want you to add one more dimension to your intelligence, and that is Observation. Observe things around you, the people around you, and you will find a different world.'

I followed his advice like a sincere student. I observed, observed and observed. The outcome? Here I am with this book. Thank you for picking it up, and happy reading!

Chapter 1

Your very own universe – wait, what?

The moment we come across the word 'universe', we think of the sky, the stars, the planets and galaxies. But this universe is common to all. It behaves the same with each and every particle that exists in it. It serves everyone equally without expecting anything in return – no demands and no complaints.

This book focuses on an entirely different universe. **The universe that is our very own creation – yes, the human-made UNIVERSE.** This is a universe that needs to be taken care of, that expects us to be at our best at all times if we expect the best from it. This personal universe of ours, is something we create unknowingly.

This self-formed universe is made up of everything that's around us – the people we surround ourselves with, the books we read, the shows we watch, the ideas we share, the habits we keep – it is made of essentially everything we come in contact with on a daily basis. Interestingly, this universe is formed while we are engrossed in life, doing things that we consider important. And we get so busy in everyday things that we fail to see what impact our universe is having on our actions, our attitudes, our thinking and our individuality as a whole.

I never gave this concept of a **self-formed** universe much thought, but when I did, it made me realise how important it is for us to pay attention this universe. I understood that each one of us has a universe that is unique to our life, and that is what makes us all so different. Everything started to connect, and as soon as I became conscious of this universe, I started receiving the signals it was trying to give me so that I could achieve what I wanted or be where I wanted to be.

Digging deeper, I found that this universe, which is all of my own, has a beautiful characteristic that the 'general' universe would never have: **I can change it!**

Yes, you and I can change our universe or, at the very least, shape it to align with our goals. This idea may seem far-fetched to you right now, but I assure you, the examples and personal experiences shared in this book will change your opinion.

***

But first, let's set your perspective right

Broadly, there are **two perspectives** of our association with the universe.

One says that we are all fighting against the Universe and therefore we have to win it over to achieve what we want. The other says that we are just a tiny part of something much bigger than ourselves, and we have to follow the rules laid down by this greater universe. This will help us shape our personal universe so that we achieve our goals.

The former perspective (that we must fight the Universe to achieve our goals) may help you motivate yourself sometimes, but it will not be of much help in shaping your life. Therefore, I request you to follow and understand this book with the latter perspective. Doing this will help you resonate with the examples in this book.

Let us now move on to understanding the components of your personal universe.

Chapter 2

What is your personal universe made of and how does it affect you?

Now that you are familiar with the concept of your own personal universe, let us understand how it impacts you and your life. I have created a list of four elements that are the most influential components of our personal universe – things that define and shape who we are and how we live.

The company we keep

Human beings are social creatures. No matter where we are located on this planet, we need other people in our lives (at least most of us do!).

According to the motivational speaker and self-help guru **Jim Rohn**, we are the average of the five people we spend most time with. During our infancy and adolescence, those five people may be our immediate family members. These are the people who give us our basic beliefs, because belief is nothing but a combination of knowledge and experience – what is taught to us growing up becomes our knowledge and what we see becomes our experience. This is how most of our beliefs are formed over time.

In every stage of life, the company we keep has a tremendous impact on our subconscious mind. Whether it's family or friends, their habits gradually start to become ours, their perspectives start to influence our own, and, before we know it, we start sharing common beliefs. Some close friends even have the same talking style.

This is one reason why children born in business families often opt for business – they grow up with that belief system. Another example could be of a person who hits their partner because they have seen it growing up. They have internalised the belief that it's the only way to show their dominance. Such people may even subconsciously adopt the same approach in other areas of their life, using force to get things done rather than building relationships through trust and respect. Our beliefs, therefore, impact us much more than we know. And how are those beliefs formed? Through the company we keep.

If you want to have control of life, start with choosing the right people to have in your life. A good person will bring out the best in you, while a bad person may influence or even force you into doing things you never wanted to (you may have experienced this in adolescence). And before you know, it turns into a trap that's impossible to get out of, no matter how hard you try.

We don't have a choice which family we are born into, but we **do have a choice** who we want to be friends with. If a friend is not helping you improve as a person, they don't deserve to be in your life. As Tim Sanders, bestselling author and public speaker, famously said, 'Your network is your net worth.' So choose wisely.

Food for thought: What type of friends do you really want to have? Because that defines what type of person you are (or will become).

Places we visit

Believe it or not, the places we visit have a big role in shaping our personality. Again, where we go often depends on the people around us – so company matters! Also, by going to the right places, we can find the people that we want to have around us.

I will share a classic example of this from my own experience. In university, I had two friends, Ronit and Akshay. Ronit was a party freak and a bit of a spoilt brat. He enjoyed smoking and drinking, and he had also tried all kinds of substances. Somewhere I felt this was an outcome of all the partying he was doing. He would make some good professional connections in those parties, but it was never of any use – neither could remember the other the next morning.

As a result, Ronit had many friends but no real buddies. Whenever any of us tried to give him a reality check, he would end the conversation with 'I'm just living in the moment bro, and I have a rich dad. So don't you worry about me!'.

Then there was Akshay – one of the most focused guys I have ever met in my life. He and Ronit were like two sides of a coin. Akshay would go to each and every seminar, exhibition and workshop on campus. That doesn't mean he didn't like partying or that he was a bore. He did party and party hard, but at the same time he made sure he didn't miss out on the important things. He always made time for events of his interest, and over time, he made a bunch of like-minded friends at these events. This opened the doors for him to be a part of a larger group who organised and attended similar events across the city.

A few months later, Akshay was approached by a journalist who was trying to build a community of eventgoers, to let more and more people know about such events and increase the footfall in those events. Today, five years later, Akshay spearheads that community, which has now turned into a successful business.

This was just one example of how the places where we spend our time affects our life.

Based on the kind of places people visit, they can be broadly divided into **two categories**:

1. Those who prefer going to places where everyone else is less educated, less successful or maybe less aware of a subject they know well. They do this as it gives them a feeling of superiority, a chance to

satisfy their ego. These people often get ahead in life by pushing or suppressing others.

2. Those who want to be in a challenging environment, where everyone is more intelligent, more experienced, more knowledgeable, or wealthier. They do this because they want to grow. The urge to be better makes them seek company that will push them out of their comfort zone and help them gain new perspectives. Such people base their success on a solid foundation of self-development and self-worth.

Food for thought: What type of places do you visit? Is it time to seek new places?

Things we read

Reading has a big impact on a person's psyche, and the irony is that we fail to notice this simple yet evident fact. Getting an education is important -- it sets your foundations right – but it takes a lot of good reading to apply that education into your real life subjectively.

Reading broadens our thinking by giving us exposure to new ideas. It enhances our understanding of right and wrong. Have you ever wondered why, even after getting the same education or studying in the same school, people grow or progress at different levels? Believe it or not, what you read plays an important role in the choices you make in life.

Reading good books, whether fiction or non-fiction, puts us in touch with our deepest thoughts and feelings.

It makes us want to ask uncomfortable questions and confront our fears. In my observation, people with a low reading quotient are often unable to have a well-rounded perspective of things. This affects not only their life choices but also their everyday decisions. If you observe closely, you will find a marked difference between people who read and those who don't read at all.

For example, a well-read person will find it difficult to do dull, mundane or repetitive work for long. They would want to break away and look for fulfilling work where their time and effort are valued.

Let me illustrate this with a real-life example. My friend Kushal's grandfather had passed away young, so Kushal's father, Manish, had to quit school to run the family store. Manish made enough money to give his children a decent education, and by the time Kushal completed his post-graduation, Manish had grown their modest neighbourhood shop into a modern grocery store.

Then he asked Kushal to join the family business. An intelligent, very well-read and highly self-aware young man, Kushal had always wanted to make a successful career on his own. Yet, on his father's insistence, he compared the revenue he would get from the store with the salary he would earn in a job, and chose to join the business.

In a matter of months, Kushal realised that this was not his cup of tea. There was nothing exciting about his work. For six months, he followed the same routine of managing the store thirteen hours a day. He would start at nine every morning and spend the entire day before the computer screen, generating bills and doing the accounts.

One day we met for a meal, and Kushal looked extremely frustrated with his life, his parents and even his own self. After a lot of nudging, he opened up about what was bothering him. He was convinced he had made a wrong choice. He felt trapped in a dull job and said that he was only doing it because of pressure from his father. This had made him resentful towards his family.

'I've always read about business tycoons and I really wanted to be one, but if I keep doing this, I think I will be stuck in this shop forever, like my father was for most of his life,' he said.

I suggested that he talk it out with his father, but he refused outright, saying he won't be an ideal son any more if he did that. There had to be another way to deal with this. We did some brainstorming and then decided that I would spend the next Sunday with him at the store and observe his routine. Together we would try and find a way out where both he and his father could be happy.

On the way back home, I kept thinking about what was happening with Kushal. The ideal son was miserable, but no one around him had a clue. He had made everyone happy, except himself. I couldn't really think of how I could help him, so I decided to wait until Sunday.

On Sunday, after spending over ten hours with Kushal, I suggested that the best way forward for him would be to hire someone for the work he was doing, so that he could shift his focus to other, more interesting aspects of the business. He had an MBA in marketing and finance, and he could use that knowledge to promote the business and increase his revenues.

Kushal loved the idea. He said he felt as if a burden had been lifted off his shoulders. He discussed the idea with his father the same night, and, to his surprise (and mine!), his father agreed to give it a try. 'Now you are all grown up and I trust your decisions,' he said.

Kushal hired a young boy to work at the shop and trained him for a week. Over time, he hired more staff. It has been two years since. He has opened another store and has done exceptionally well in terms of turning a profit and marketing the business. And, he hasn't stopped reading!

Food for thought: If you have a friend stuck in a similar conundrum, maybe you need to ask them, 'What are you reading?'

Things we watch

You may agree that a person's Netflix suggestions or their google search history can tell a lot about their personality. In fact, what we watch can mould our personality to such an extent over time that we won't even know it has happened.

No matter on which device or platform you use, their artificial intelligence is designed to show or suggest you more content on the same topics. To better understand this, go to your YouTube now and search for the best hip-hop songs of 2020. Watch four to five of those videos, and the next time you are back, your feed will show you more videos on the same topic. Now imagine this multiplying effect on your brain and hence on your personality.

There are so many studies out there that show that video has a much greater impact on us than text or audio, because visual information is far easier to absorb and retain than written or oral communication. This is why sometimes we remember the face of a person but forget their name, or why we remember the scenes but not so much the dialogues from films we watched years ago. This also explains why everyone today is so focused on producing visual content.

The degree of impact of what we watch can be seen in a very recent example from the early stages of the Coronavirus pandemic. In a country as advanced as the US, some people put out pretty convincing videos on social media that the virus was a hoax. As a result, millions didn't start taking the necessary precautions until some serious damage had been done. See how the fake videos managed to influence millions of educated people?

If you are still not convinced as to how much visual content can impact us, I recommend that you watch the documentary *The Social Dilemma* on Netflix. Some of the facts will blow your mind. In fact the pandemic example I used above is from this documentary itself.

Today we are constantly bombarded with videos on every topic possible, and therefore, it is all the more critical to choose what we watch. Knowing how these choices affect your personality and your brain will help you choose more wisely.

Food for thought: Are you spending your screen time on the right stuff or just the good stuff?

***

Now that you know what affects your universe, you can slowly and steadily work on fine-tuning these components to your advantage. Moving on, there are certain gifts that help us notice and trace the signals the universe is trying to send us. When you are tuned in to these gifts and powers, you will better understand your self-formed universe and how it affects you.

Chapter 3

Gifts from the universe

I feel now we are quite on the same page, but before going any further, I wish to draw your attention to affirmation (or gratitude).

Starting today, create a morning ritual: Think of all that you are grateful for and thank the almighty for all the boons and bounties in your life. Be grateful for all that you have, all your privileges (it can be something as simple as having a concrete structure over your head).

Let the words 'Think and Thank' be engraved in your heart, just as they are inscribed on the walls of a church. This simple practice will help you start your day with a positive attitude and energise you for the day ahead. And it will gradually wean you off a complaining attitude, because **you can't be grateful and complaining at the same time.**

Everything we possess, whether material or non-material, we owe it to the Universe. You and I can't deny the fact that the universe is full of gifts and surprises. Being born on earth and that too as a human is certainly one of the gifts that this universe has showered on us.

Now I am about to disclose some unique gifts that human beings enjoy the most among all species. These gifts are available to each and every individual on earth, irrespective of their gender, faith, location, income, beliefs or habits. Despite these gifts being available to all of us, it's how we use them that makes us different from each other.

Unfortunately, we either fail to realise that we have these gifts, or we misuse them. It's funny how we often realise the worth of these gifts only after we have lost them – in case you don't believe it, I will help you see how all of us do this.

So, before I tell you how to make your universe favourable and make the most out of it, let us first learn what this universe has gifted us and how can we use these powers to enhance our lives.

The body

The human body, made up of over 100 trillion cells, is the most complex and advanced of all species on the planet. It is incredibly flexible and is able to move in a thousand ways, all thanks to the 320 pairs of skeletal muscles. If you compare trait by trait, you will find some species better than humans; for example, a tiger can run faster; fish can swim better and longer. But if you view the human body as a complete package, you will have to agree that it is truly a remarkable creation.

Your body is one of the very few things on this planet that gets better the more you use it. The more you work on your body, the more it works for you. Yes, the human body is meant for movement. Lack of movement attracts disease. Therefore, movement is essential if you want your body to respond and operate better and use it to its maximum potential.

If you want your body to listen to you, you will have to work hard on it. The best thing is that you can mould your body the way you want. People like the athlete David Goggins, often called the toughest man on earth, have taught us that if properly trained, our body can do things most people can't even imagine.

Your body is a priceless gift, and when it is in top shape, you will start looking at your life differently and that will itself solve a number of your problems – trust me, because I have been there!

However, to perform at its best, the human body needs support from the other amazing gift given to us by the universe.

This marvel is called the **human brain**, which has no match in the world, or may I say the universe, which is why I consider it the second unique gift the universe has showered on us humans.

The brain

The human brain is the prime reason we are considered the most evolved species on the planet. The brain is 1/50th of our body mass but consumes a staggering 1/5th of the calories we use for energy, so, clearly, we are what we eat!

No other species in the universe can match the computational power of the human brain. In his book *The Singularity Is Near*, Ray Kurzweil estimated that a $1,000 computer in 2020 will have the same processing power as that of the human brain, and that by 2045 the intelligence of a computer will exceed the intelligence of humans.[1]

Isn't that amazing?

There is yet another fascinating power of the human brain, called **Metacognition**, which means thinking about thinking. This can be thinking about your own or another person's thinking.

Let me illustrate this with an example. Suppose you are solving a math problem and are unable to solve it the first time. Now when you try a second time, you are also simultaneously thinking of the thought process you had the first time, so that you don't repeat the same mistakes. Therefore, at this point, you are thinking about your own thinking.

Now, imagine you have to launch a new product in the market. You will have to think like a potential customer in order to make your product or service a success, because people's buying patterns resonate directly with their psyche, other things being constant.

For instance, once I went for an interview at a company that provided homestays. I was asked where I

---

[1] https://www.eitdigital.eu/news-events/blog/article/what-is-the-computational-power-of-our-brain

thought they could find potential customers or what type of travellers, would like to book a homestay instead of a hotel. All thanks to my Metacognition power, I was able to think like a potential homestay customer and give an answer that pleased the interviewer. Needless to say, I got the job.

The comfort parody

In addition to these qualities, the human brain has a unique trait that can act as a double-edged sword, if not used strategically.

Our brain always has a tactical advantage over us. It knows our weaknesses, insecurities and the deep, dark lies we tell ourselves. So the moment we try to step out of our comfort zone, it starts to push us in the opposite direction, to the familiar and comfortable. This is because our brain is designed for survival, not success.

Ever wondered why your mind wanders to other activities (like playing, binge-watching shows, meeting friends or taking a nap) whenever you sit to study for an important project or an exam? Or why you want to leave it all and run to the mountains whenever you are stuck at a boring corporate party? Or, going back in time, why you would wake up late for school but were always on time for play. This, my friend, is our brain doing the Comfort Parody.

I know, now you are probably saying, 'It wasn't me! It was my brain!'

It was indeed.

But this comfort parody is what keeps us from being the best we can be. If you want to be somewhere in life, you will need to step away from this comfort parody, and the best way to do this is to train your mind to be comfortable in the most uncomfortable situations, to make a habit of going one step further when your mind tells you to stop. Yes, you can do it with practice and perseverance. All the great athletes, artists and leaders step in and out of their comfort zone over and over again, proving that there is no limit to what a person can achieve, if they learn how to conquer their mind.

The third gift from the Universe is that we are all unique in our own ways.

Uniqueness

Human species is the most diversified in the world. Even though we all are blessed with the same physical attributes, we are all so different. Even two exactly identical twins are not the same, because they have different brains that make them to think and act differently. This, in my view, is yet another invaluable gift from the universe.

But the irony is that instead of celebrating this gift, we are always comparing ourselves with others. In fact, we are taught comparison from our very childhood. Someone else's child is more beautiful, more intelligent, more obedient. Even our education system thrives on comparison by way of marks, position in class and so on.

Teachers often tend to appreciate students who are obedient and dislike those who are not. Unfortunately, we are never taught to ask, did everyone who is successful always follow the rules? Do people who always follow the rules succeed for sure? The people we consider smart and successful today – did they always get good marks in academics?

Yes, we need educational reforms, but what we need more as a society is a reform in our mindset. We need to develop appreciation for the fact that everyone is uniquely different and will do things differently. Even children born and raised in the same family and in the same environment grow up to have wildly different personalities. Then how can we expect people coming from entirely different backgrounds to learn, work or behave in the same manner?

The problem lies in our belief that ours is the only way to get things done. This is how we limit our thoughts and hence our universe. What we should be doing instead is observe and analyse different ways of doing the same thing, and then use that knowledge to create permutations and combinations that will give us the desired output in the most productive way.

We need to get rid of the mindset of always focusing on others' shortcomings. We all have imperfections, but along with these imperfections the universe has blessed each one of us with at least one unique quality. This quality is what will take us forward; it is what will overpower our imperfections.

Our real work lies in finding this quality and nurturing it. The more you nurture it, the more it will help you stand out in your personal and professional life. And believe me, today it is much easier to nurture a unique quality or skill than it was, say, ten years ago – all thanks to the exposure we all have through the internet.

So go, get it all. Find what you are good at – or something that you love doing, even if you are not great at it – because you have plenty of time to nurture what you love doing. If you need help figuring it out, ask your family and close friends the quality they like most in you. What, according to them, do you have that others don't?

The universe has left this work to you: to discover this quality within you. Once you find it, the universe will kneel to you, and the more you nurture this quality, the more inspired you will feel.

If you are one of those who think they don't have any quality in them (though I doubt there is anyone like that on this planet), consider yourself lucky, because you can develop any quality you wish to have. Yes, you can! It may take time and effort to acquire your unique gift, but it is possible. So go all in, because that's the only way to distinguish yourself from others.

Now, let us see what powers your universe has and how you can use those powers to achieve your dreams.

Chapter 4

The powers of your universe

The universe has numerous powers that help and guide us in various ways. These powers have a big impact on our lives, though we often fail to notice this because our attention is focused on acquiring 'worldly' powers by influence, recognition or force.

The powers of our self-formed universe are so impactful that they can make or break our lives. My motive is to bring these powers to your notice so that you can use them to your advantage, because, in order to use these powers, you must first be aware that they do exist.

The power of thoughts

Before we dive into the power of thoughts, let me explain the formation of thoughts – that is, how thoughts are formed and whether we have any control over the process.

How do you know what you know?

Thoughts are nothing but our belief about a particular thing, and belief comes from a combination of Knowledge and Experience (this is my belief!).

Now why did I say knowledge *and* experience and not knowledge or experience alone? Because sometimes our knowledge of something can be challenged by our experience of that thing or activity, and vice versa. In other words, our experience of something may not turn out to be exactly what we knew about it.

Here's an example: Your friend couldn't stop raving about a new restaurant in town, but when you went there, the food was pathetic, the service average. Now, according to your knowledge the food should have been great, but your experience was entirely different. You decided that you will not recommend the place to anyone. The experience shaped a new belief in you about that restaurant that is entirely different from that of your friend.

Now, if you share your experience with your friend, he will find it hard to believe, as he had a positive experience at the same place. So, even though you both had the same knowledge, your experiences affected your perception and therefore your beliefs.

Our life experiences have shaped us into the people we are today. This is how children raised in the same environment can have entirely different personalities – they may have received the same knowledge growing up, but their experiences could be entirely different from each other.

This is what makes every individual different, and this is why I often say that everyone is right in what they do – they do it because they believe it to be right at that point of time. Any guilt, or introspection, will come only when there is a change in that belief.

Knowledge + Experiences → Beliefs → Thoughts → Personality

By now it is clear that what we take in shapes our thoughts, and by changing this input, we can change our thoughts whenever we want.

Of course, you will have negative experiences that will trigger negative thoughts, but just like you throw your trash into the bin, you can learn to let go of negative thoughts as soon as they cross your mind. This is not easy, I must add. It is a conscious practice that needs commitment, but you get better with time.

Here's a fact if you are still not convinced about the power of thoughts: **The damage done by a negative thought is far greater than the repair made by a positive thought.** According to Christine Porath (renowned author, speaker and associate professor of management at Georgetown University and Harvard University), negativity is four to seven times more powerful than positivity.[2]

So, it is very important to train our minds to avoid negative thoughts.

---

[2] https://www.eitdigital.eu/news-events/blog/article/what-is-the-computational-power-of-our-brain

'The Mind is everything. What you think, you become,' said Gautama Buddha. I am a strong believer of this, because every single thing we do in our lives was once a thought that came to our mind before we turned it into action. This means that we have the power to turn any thought into reality. For instance, I would never have been able to write this book if I had never thought of it.

Every event that is happening with or around you is shaping your thoughts and, in turn, your personality. Believe me when I say that you can achieve anything in your life just by strengthening your thought process – I have experienced this more than once.

You can read more on this in *The Secret*, the widely acclaimed masterpiece by Paulo Coelho. I love this book and I am sure you will like it too.

Now that you have gained a fair understanding of the power of your thoughts, follow all the steps in Chapter 2 ('What is Your Personal Universe Made of, and How Does that Affect You?') and let's build a better world by shaping ourselves into better human beings.

The power of doing (karma)

'A man is born alone and dies alone; and he experiences the good and bad consequences of his karma alone; and he goes alone to hell or the Supreme abode,' said Chanakya, the ancient Indian teacher, thinker and philosopher.

Karma has been perceived in many different ways by different traditions and faiths. People sometimes have different opinions about Karma, but if you observe deeply, you will find that the words used may be different, but the underlying context always remains the same.

There is absolutely nothing wrong in having your own definition of Karma, as long as it serves its purpose – of keeping you from hurting or harming anyone. I firmly believe that every action we take is Karma, and that every action will have consequences, either positive or negative, depending on the intent or type of action. This is the definition that most resonates with me, and I hope it will help you form your own.

Everything we do has many implications. We may succeed in hiding our deeds from people, but the universe will know, and it will pay us back sooner or later. If you help someone in need, you will certainly get help when you need it. The fruits of your actions will be received in this life only, sometimes sooner than expected.

This is the universe's power of giving back. As you sow, so shall you reap!

There's also a scientific way to understand this: If we have good intentions and we really want to serve others, we will generate an ocean of positive thoughts in our subconscious mind. We will see positivity in everything that happens to us, because our subconscious mind knows that, since we have done no wrong, nothing wrong will happen to us. **A person of this mindset believes that everything happens for good.**

Similarly, when we intentionally do something wrong for our benefit, our subconscious mind will be flooded with negative thoughts, because somewhere deep down we are acutely aware of the intention behind our actions. And when life comes full circle, we will know that everything wrong happening to us is because we did the same to someone.

In a nutshell, we can say that **our karma and our thoughts are interconnected**. Good karma leads to good thoughts and bad karma brings bad thoughts, and vice versa. It's an eternal cycle that dictates what we experience and how we live. It is, therefore, karma that helps in maintaining the balance in the universe.

Ending this section with the words of my favourite singer and songwriter, Kesha: 'I believe in karma, and I believe if you put out positive vibes to everybody, that's all you are going to get back.'

Now, let's move on to the third power of the universe.

The power of abundance

You may be familiar with the Law of Attraction, which states that we have the power to attract whatever we desire in life.

What if I told you there is a complementary power to the law of attraction?

It is the Law of Abundance. Unfortunately, not many people are aware of this power, even though it is this power that enables us to practise the law of attraction and helps us get what we want from life and from the universe. It is the law of abundance that helps us dream beyond our capabilities.

Let me simplify this. According to the law of abundance, there is an unlimited source of everything we need or could ever ask for. The Sun has enough light for each and every corner of the world. Nature has enough air for every living being to breathe. There is going to be enough food for all species to survive, no matter how populated the world gets. There are numerous other examples that prove the existence of the law of abundance.

I am a firm believer of the law of abundance, and, in my view, **lack of resources is a myth. The only truth is the lack of resourcefulness.**

Everything is available to us at all times – we just need to focus our energy on what we want and it will come our way. For instance, when I shared the idea of writing this book with a friend, he said that I could never be a successful writer as the world already has too many writers. Of course I did not agree with him or you would not be reading this book.

The universe is truly without limitation, and it is abundantly giving. When we wish for something earnestly, we create infinite energy that aligns us with the law of abundance and turns that wish into reality. It is due to this very abundance that each one of us gets a chance to pursue our dreams.

Do you ever think about how your universe is so much different from the universe of those who lived in the 1950s or '60s? They did not have much of what we have today, but they dreamed of those things, summoned them and made them available for future generations.

Thus, the law of abundance ensures that whatever is thought of is created in the universe, for better or worse. Now let us take a moment to thank our previous generations for all that they created for us by dreaming big and making it happen.

The power of reversal

I don't know if anyone else has experienced or noticed this power. I have, and I firmly believe in its existence.

The power of reversal is essentially the universe's power of taking back.

Sometimes we see that some people get what they want by pure luck or chance, or through inheritance. It could be an opportunity, a position or even a fortune. An untalented person gets through an audition; a well-connected person's son or daughter gets an (unfair) advantage over others; an undeserving person gets access to opportunities others could kill for.

This happens quite often around us, but have you ever noticed that this stroke of luck, chance or whatsoever you may call it only gets these people in the door. If they want to retain these positions or opportunities, they will have to prove their worth to the universe.

Finding Your Own Universe

If the universe does not find you deserving of its gifts, it may take them back, whether you got them through luck or hard work. Those of us who have found extraordinary success know that the only way we get to keep what we have is by respecting and valuing it. The moment we start taking anything for granted, we can start counting days before it is snatched away from us. Perhaps this is why Jeff Bezos, the richest person in the world, continues to show up for work every day.

Why does this happen? Why does the universe engage in this give and take?

Because there is someone somewhere more hard-working and more deserving, who is hustling to get what we have, and the universe has a responsibility towards that person too.

So how do you keep the universe from taking back what it gave you? It's simple. If you honestly apply every other power of the universe in your life, the power of reversal automatically goes into the bin.

Part II

Before proceeding to how to make your universe favourable – let me tell you why a favourable universe is needed at all. No matter how good your intentions or actions are, if your surroundings or your environment don't support you, these actions would not be as fruitful as they could be in a favourable universe.

For instance, you will struggle to quit smoking in an environment where the people that you live with, or see every day, are always smoking. On the other hand, it would be much easier to quit if you are the only smoker in your circle of friends, who repeatedly condemn you for the habit.

I want to share one more example of an unsupportive environment, from my own life. I have always been a fan of healthy eating and healthy living. When I turned twenty, I created a meal plan where I had to eat clean every day, with one cheat day every week. I started on an absolutely positive note, sure that I could make it happen. At the time I was sharing a flat with four friends who were all big-time foodies (as they like to call themselves). They would order tempting food every other day, and sometimes I would end up cheating twice in a single day, forget once a week. My plan to live healthier fell flat and I even turned bitter towards my roomies for a while.

I am certainly not saying that we should blame all our failures on others or on the universe, but our environment clearly has a big impact on our thoughts and actions. If not, there would be no need for rehabilitation centres or wellness retreats. Of course, the degree of impact varies from person to person, but we can completely negate this impact by being conscious with our choices. A favourable and supportive universe will help us achieve the greatest of our potential, and we are the ones who will have to create that universe.

Remember:

Environment + Thoughts + Action = Results

Chapter 5

How to make your universe favourable

Since you are the creator of your personal universe, you are the only one who can make it favourable. A favourable universe is one that supports you in accomplishing your goals. In such a universe, everything around you motivates you and helps you go at the things you want with full force. There is no negativity to stop you and no one telling you that you can't do it.

But the question is, how do we create a favourable universe?

The favourable universe consists of everything working in your favour. As explained in Chapter 2, 'What is Your Personal Universe Made of, and How Does it Affect You?', you can have the best people around you, go to the best places, and read and watch the best of things – but that's only half the work done. The remaining half is solely in your hands.

Having the best of everything around you will not get you what you want – you will have to work for it. You will have to figure out the perfect mix that brings out the best in you.

This can be achieved by simple trial and error. For instance, some people work better at night, some early in the morning and yet others are at their best during the day. Find the best time for you, when you are most productive or creative, and then allocate the most important tasks of the day to that time. As for me, I found that I am more creative around midnight, so I make sure I write only around this time. One of my friends believes that he gets his best ideas in the shower – some may find it silly but it works for him!

This really works! Try it and watch the magic happen.

Similarly, find an environment that suits you best, one that helps you work to the best of your abilities. Do you like working in a closed room or in an open space? Do you get nervous when someone pressurises you to do something, or are you at your best under pressure? Do you need guidance to work efficiently, or can you do just as well without it?

Find the answers to these questions and many more that you believe can help you extract the best out of you. When you have these answers, turn them into habits, and soon you will have your most favourable universe around you.

I must add that you can find these answers only if you are patient enough to observe your behaviour deeply and continuously.

One last thing! It is completely all right to make amendments to your universe if you feel that it's no more working in your favour. For example, if you feel that you need to change your work environment, change it. However, be practical and understand that it doesn't make sense to change something today just because it didn't work for you yesterday. Give it time. If you feel the same even after, say, two weeks, go ahead and make the change.

Remember, you are the only one who can detect any misalignments in your universe and tweak them in your favour.

If you feel that your universe is already favourable, then believe me, my friend, you are truly blessed. You can achieve anything if you put your heart and mind to it.

Now, let's see how we should handle this invaluable universe we have created.

Chapter 6

Etiquette towards a favourable universe

'Handle with care' – that's the tag that comes along with your favourable universe. Just like we need to have a certain behaviour or etiquette towards people or things we want in our lives, we need to do the same with our universe – we need to treat it well.

If you own a car, for example, you go to great lengths to make sure it runs at peak performance – you get it serviced on time, drive under a certain speed for good mileage, and so on. You display etiquette towards an inanimate object to keep it in good shape.

Similarly, if you have a relationship or an individual that you don't want to lose, you do everything – care for them, be there for them, bring them a meaningful gift – to nurture the relationship and make it last as long as you can.

Don'ts for a favourable universe

Once you have made so much effort to create a favourable universe, I am sure you would want it to last as long as it can. There are certain don'ts that you need to follow to ensure this.

Don't overthink

We have already discussed how powerful the human brain is and how lucky we are to have it. However, this brain also has the power to turn our lives upside down, even if everything is perfect in our outer universe.

The brain has a unique power that can destroy you, and **this destructive power is called overthinking.**

Overthinking literally stops you from doing anything, because even if you think the best of ideas and make the best plans, overthinking will compel you to into believing that something will go wrong.

There will always be things that you can't control – overthinking simply means you are constantly worrying about these uncontrollable things, when you know that you can do little or nothing about them. Someone rightly said, analysis leads to paralysis!

Up next I discuss how to remove fear or cope with it. We can apply the same principles whenever we are trapped in overthinking, because overthinking, I believe, is the root of most of our fears.

I remember talking to a friend's father recently, who runs a successful automobile component manufacturing business, with customers all over the country. He talked about how tough it is to do business in these times. He said that he's constantly worried about incurring losses, which is taking a toll on his health.

I listened to him intently, then asked what stressed him most about his business. I was quite surprised by what he said. It was not sales, not staff, not cash flow, but something that was quite beyond his control.

'No matter to which part of the country I'm delivering, but throughout the transit of my goods I'm extremely tensed that something or other will happen to my stock,' he said. 'Sometimes I have these dreams about my stock being seized by some officials on the way, although my paperwork is always impeccable. Or I worry that the truck will catch fire, though all my shipments are insured.

'Sometimes I have nightmares about robberies and accidents,' he concluded, wiping the sweat off his palms with a crisp white handkerchief.

I didn't have much to say to him, but I thought about it later. This man knew he was being unreasonably anxious, yet he was unable to stop himself. Do you think he had lost it? Or was it a simple case of over-worrying?

In my view, he was not overly worried, but there was problem with his fear setting. **Fear setting** (discussed later) plays a crucial role in overcoming any fear, which brings me to the next *don't* for a favourable universe. Here I explain how fear works and how you can do your fear setting in a way that fear will no longer haunt you.

Don't fear

Fear is not real. Yes, I mean it. No matter how often or how strongly you feel it, I want you to remember that fear is just an illusion.

Let me put it another way. When you are fearful you are always thinking in the past or in the future. You are thinking of something that doesn't really exist in the present. Please read that again. Fear is always followed by 'what if'. You are always thinking, what if I fail again? What if I can't make it? What if I waste a few precious years of my life and still don't make it?

In the words of the great artist, writer and educator J. Ruth Gendler, 'Fear has a large shadow, but he himself is small.' Recall the last time you ended up not doing something because of fear. You probably regretted it later. On the other hand, if you did do something in spite of being scared, you may have looked back and thought how foolish it was to be so scared. One thing is sure: the more we face our fears the stronger it makes us.

In my experience, if there is one thing that's more dangerous than an actual fear, it is the fear of fear itself. To eliminate fear we must not ask ourselves how to remove fear; we should ask what fear is. We need to try and understand fear, because anything that can be understood can be managed. Everyone has different ways to cope with their fears. Some tricks might work for certain people and for certain type of fears only.

I was looking for a universal method to control fear, one that is easy to understand and can work in almost all scenarios. That's when I came across a podcast by Timothy Ferriss,[3] one of my all-time favourite authors who has written many bestselling self-help books; *The 4-Hour Work week*, *The 4-Hour Body*, *Tools of Titans*, to name a few.

I urge everyone reading this book to listen to at least one episode of his podcast, *The Tim Ferriss Show*.

In one episode, Ferris talks about stoicism. He says: 'The simple meaning of stoicism is the quality or practice of enduring a crisis without complaining or showing emotion. People who know stoicism use it as a comprehensive system for doing a lot of things. The chief among them is to train oneself to separate what can be controlled from what cannot be controlled, and then develop a habit of focusing specifically on all that is in one's control.'

Practising stoicism can reduce emotional reactivity, which can prove to be a superpower when dealing with life's challenges.

In the case of my friend's father, stoicism can help him overcome his crippling anxiety over things he cannot control and help him focus on other aspects of his life, such as his health.

---

3   https://open.spotify.com/episode/328LiqvFaxQli3FSv9IG X7?si=xzuv2AanTOGl-hPsbxZ9FA

Fear can weaken your perfectly favourable universe. So how do you stop being scared of fear and learn to look it in the eye?

In his podcast, Ferris refers to an exercise called Premeditatio Malorum: the premeditation of evils. Using this stoic meditation as a reference, he discusses a three-part exercise, described below.

The first part, FEAR SETTING, is all about facing your fears in black-and-white

It has three steps.

STEP 1: What if I...

Here you have to write down whatever you are fearful of or whatever is causing you anxiety, or something that you have been putting off for a while. It could be anything, from taking up a new job, venturing into business, or asking someone out.

Next, write down all the worst-case scenarios that could happen if you took that step. Start with 'What if I...' and make a list of all that could go wrong if you took the plunge.

Let me give you my example. At one point, I was terrified at the idea of writing a book. One day I wrote down fifteen points that were holding me back from penning my first few words; for example, who's going to read a book about the universe from a person who hasn't experienced enough life yet? What if I finish writing but can't find a publisher?

STEP 2: What can I...

Here you write down all that you can do to prevent those worst-case events from happening, or to at least reduce their likelihood. For instance, with regard to my fear of not being able to find a publisher, I figured that I will always have the option to self-publish.

STEP 3: How will I...

This is the repairing stage. If the worst actually happens, what would you do to repair the damage? Or, who could you ask for help?

In my case, there was a possibility that, upon self-publishing, my book may find no readers. I decided that if that happens, I will take a short vacation, repair my ego and take the time to think whether I want to invest more time in improving my craft or quit writing altogether.

The best way to do this part of the exercise is to find people who have been through the same situation and learn what they did when failure struck.

The second part is about playing against your fears.

Here you need to write down what may be the benefits of attempting what you are fearful of. What skills could you acquire on the way? How would the decision impact you emotionally, professionally, financially? Spend at least fifteen to twenty minutes on this exercise.

When I did this exercise, I could weigh the benefits of writing a book against not writing one. I came to the conclusion that even the worst-case scenario after writing the book will leave me a better individual than I am today. I would gain deep knowledge of a subject of my interest, and I would have more confidence in my writing than ever before. All in all, the chances of me gaining something from it were more than losing

To my surprise, the outcome has been way better than I imagined. Here you are reading this book, because of that one decision I took.

The third and final part is all about the cost of inaction.

We humans are exceptionally talented when it comes to thinking about what might go wrong if we tried something new. But how often do we consider the true cost of not trying at all and being stuck in the same place for years?

Here is what you should ask yourself when pessimistic thoughts cloud your mind: What if I avoid this action or decision? What will my life look like in a month or a year from now?

Think critically and write down honest answers to these questions.

When I did this exercise, I figured that it was better to start writing anyway, because it would be somewhat better than not writing at all. Today I'm glad I made that choice.

The next time you fear something, use this framework and you will find that most of the times, **what fear does is that it makes you choose inaction.** Let me remind you, my friend, that any action is better than inaction.

Don't regret

Regret is the most dangerous thing to hold on to. We have to understand that regret is always related to the past, and no matter how much we have advanced in science, we are yet to invent a way to travel back in time and fix things.

Moreover, why regret something when the decision you made or the action you took *felt right at that moment*? Isn't that why you made that choice in the first place? Rather than grieving over past mistakes, review them critically, learn what went wrong, and resolve never to repeat the same mistakes again.

Remember, if you keep looking back, the favourable universe you have created with so much effort will start to lose its power. It needs your attention, and for that you have to live in the **present**.

Don't compare or judge

Comparing yourself to anyone apart from your own self is a futile exercise. You should not compare, simply because it will never be a fair comparison!

Each one of us is *different*. We can compare apples to apples, not apples to oranges. So even when two people have the exact same resources, they won't get the same results.

When you find yourself falling prey to comparison, remind yourself that the universe has a unique plan for you, and for everyone else, for that matter. Which is why some people marry at an age when others are still figuring out their career options, and some die young and successful while others think they wasted their entire lives and did nothing worthwhile.

Always remember, you are neither ahead of anyone nor behind. You are growing at your *own pace*, and so is everyone else.

Chapter 7

Challenges from your universe (after you have made it favourable)

Now that your universe is favourable and you are on your way to success, you may still face some challenges. The **universe will test** how badly you want something, and passing this test won't be easy because your current mindset will resist these challenges with full force.

I have seen many who lust for success others have found, but are not willing to take on challenges those others may have overcome in their journey. We need to remember that anything that comes without challenges is either not worth it or won't last long. Moreover, challenges make success much more delectable.

It's not that these challenges did not exist before you had a favourable universe – they did, but it would have been wrong to call them challenges. They were problems – problems without solutions.

Let's discuss these challenges and how to overcome them.

You will feel lost

Feeling lost is as real as feeling happy, sad or emotional, so we should not be afraid of this feeling. It's okay to feel lost sometimes. It's okay to not be able to figure out everything every time. I say this because everyone on their journey up feels lost at times. Everyone gets butterflies in the belly every now and then, wondering whether what they are doing is worth their time and effort.

Does feeling lost mean you are doing something wrong or unachievable? Certainly not. Everything is achievable in this universe. Things that seem impossible right now may well be achieved five or ten years from now (remember the law of abundance?).

So what should you do when you feel lost? First of all, understand that it's a temporary feeling. Second, it's a myth that only those who are in the process of being successful feel lost – even the most successful people feel this way sometimes.

Just like the body, the mind also gets tired. And this can happen frequently when you are blindly following your passion or your dream, forgetting that there's a lot more in life that needs your time and attention.

To overcome this state of mind, give yourself some space by stepping away from the task or work you have been doing for a long time (long enough that you have blocked your mind from thinking about anything else).

Even if this means going away from that environment for some time, do that.

You are human, so it's absolutely all right to feel overwhelmed at times, but if you always have the same feelings towards anything or anyone, it's a sign of humanity dying inside you.

Feeling lost all the time is a sign that you need a break. Get away, take the time to rejuvenate, so that you can look at your life and your work with a fresh perspective.

You will want to quit

In most achiever stories you will find one of two things: success came their way either when they were least expecting it (of course after giving it all they could) or when they had already lost hope.

If you have ever worked out at the gym, you may have seen that the last three reps after you simply want to quit are the hardest but also the most rewarding than the first ten. It's as if the universe is testing your patience after you have passed the test of hard work.

So, if you are on the verge of quitting something that was all you wanted once, don't do it yet. **It's just the universe testing your nerve.** Give your all to those last few reps, and life will be good soon.

You will have to sacrifice a lot

Yet again you missed the Saturday hangout with your friends. Don't you worry! And be prepared to sacrifice even more until you reach a point where missing a party will stop feeling like a sacrifice at all.

Learn to say NO, even if it hurts someone, because this hurt is temporary. But by saying yes to everything that comes your way, you will hurt your own self, and this hurt will last longer than the hurt of saying no.

When you choose to walk the path to your dreams, you will have to sacrifice your comfort, your sleep, maybe even some of your friends, but believe me, it will all be worth it in the end. That's how life is: we have to let go of some things to be able to gain something greater in life.

You may find it difficult to believe this now, and that's understandable, but once you are there, once you have achieved what you wanted and look back, all those sacrifices will seem necessary – in fact, you may even stop calling them sacrifices, because with your success you have justified every choice you made to reach where you are today.

You are finally convinced that **what you didn't do was equally important as what you did to be where you are.**

You will struggle with discipline

First, I would like to clear the difference between being disciplined and being punctual. Being punctual means doing the same thing at the same time every day; for example, waking up at six every morning. Whereas being disciplined has a broader definition. It means that you are doing something every day but not necessarily at the same time; for instance, I work out every day whenever I get time, sometimes even late at night.

With this clear distinction between the two, you will find that being disciplined is far easier than being punctual. But you may still face problems in having a disciplined life. What I suggest is to start slow and steady. Don't go all in at once. Obviously, it will be difficult in the beginning, or should I put it this way: it will be difficult only in the beginning.

Let's say that you want to lose weight but you think that you don't have the time to work out (mind me, that's what you think). To begin with, start taking out five minutes initially to work on your body; increase it to ten, then twenty, and gradually it will be a part of your routine like anything else. You will not have to make special effort to include exercise in your routine. The transformation you will experience will make you want to do more, and your progress will soon be on autopilot.

In essence, whatever may be your dream, if you want to make it true in this lifetime, embrace the pain of discipline – because it's always better than the pain of regret.

You will feel lonely

If you want to be successful in the long run, you will have to learn to be happy alone. Believe me, and I say this from experience, your family is your only constant and permanent companion. Many who claim to be your best friends will vanish in hard times. Don't be surprised if your partner, too, turns their back on you.

My intention here is not to demotivate you but to make you aware of the harsh realities of life.

When you are working hard for your dream, only those who understand you will stay by your side, because they know that you are not avoiding them but only prioritising your time to achieve something great.

As they say, in life we never lose friends, we only learn *who the true ones are.* All this is a part of the process, so don't lose heart. I lost plenty of my so-called friends in my pursuit of success. But, although I knew this would happen, I still felt alone. I had no one to talk to or to share my feelings with. But that didn't pull me back. Rather, it pushed me further because I was sure that I was on the right track. I was sure that I could win back all my friends and much more, but time, once wasted, could never be brought back.

It will take longer than you expected

This may not hold true for everyone or every situation, but it will often take longer to achieve your goal than you expected. There will be hurdles that you did not or could not foresee. Problems that you never considered would crop up out of nowhere. The people you wanted to meet and the opportunities you wanted to seize may not be available when you need them most.

Life is an ongoing saga of changes and uncertainties, so don't be disheartened when things take longer than expected. Don't feel low when you underachieve anything. What's most important is to keep moving – **it doesn't matter if you are running or crawling as long as you are going in the right direction.**

There will be many, many distractions

Focus is the key, my friend. And it's not just a word but a feeling, a lifestyle, a mindset that few are able to achieve. In these times, when so much is screaming for our attention, focusing has become way harder than it was probably a decade or two ago.

To add to that, most of us have a wrong or incomplete definition of focus. **Focus not only means doing the right thing to reach your goal, but also avoiding all that distracts you from doing the right thing.** As aptly put by the gaming legend John Carmack, 'Focus is a matter of deciding what things you're not going to do.'

If you learn to control your mind, you will be able to eliminate everything that keeps you from doing your most important tasks. Here are a few tips to help you stay focused.

How to build focus

Avoid multitasking

Multitasking is the new cool. Almost everyone multitasks these days, thinking that it will help them do more in less time. But believe me, **multitasking is a myth**.

The ego in you may counter this fact, because you have seen that you can easily do two things at a time. You can walk while you talk, chew while you read, watch while you think.

However, if you notice, you can't do two things at once when both of them demand your complete attention or focus. You can't drive and talk on your phone (I know many of us do it all the time, but we also know that it takes away our focus from the road).

The fact is, whenever we focus on more than one thing at a time, our attention bounces back and forth. As a result, we are not able to do either of the tasks with 100% accuracy or efficiency.

It's not that we are short of time – it's just that we have a strong need to do too many things at once. But, as the acclaimed photographer and speaker Steve Uzzell said, 'Multitasking is merely the opportunity to screw up more than one thing at a time.'

So, if you want to develop focus, delete *multitasking* from your dictionary.

Try meditation

In my experience, meditation is the most effective way to build focus. Those who meditate are able to focus on a task relatively longer than those who don't. I have personally experienced the multiple benefits of meditation, so I request you to at least try it out.

In the words of **Zen Master** Thich Nhat Hanh, 'Meditation can help us embrace our worries, our fear, our anger; and that is very healing. We let our own natural capacity of healing do the work.'

Yes, it may be difficult in the beginning, but eventually you will start enjoying it. Start with as little as five minutes and gradually build up your practice. No matter which meditation technique or process you follow, the ultimate goal is one – to enhance your focus.

Develop a focusing habit

It happens often that we are physically at one place but mentally somewhere else. Studies show that we spend about 2.1 hours every day in distraction, and it takes us 21 minutes to refocus. Imagine how much more productive we can be if we learn to control our minds and focus on the present moment!

It would not be wrong to say that we are living in an era where focus is valued more than intelligence, all thanks to social media and games and gadgets. To help you find your focus, I would like you to take out some time for *you*. Spend time in solitude, with no devices around. Try to avoid of the compulsion to check your phone every other minute.

A focusing habit I absolutely love is the one from Robin Sharma, one of the world's top leadership experts. It's called the **90/90/1 Rule**.[4]

---

4 https://www.youtube.com/watch?v=cshVfS2LXm0&list=WL&index=45

I am a lifelong fan of this formula, because it is the reason I was able to complete this book. Here's how it goes.

For the next 90 days, spend the first 90 minutes of your day doing one thing that you think can be a game changer for your life. Focus on the greatest opportunity you are after and spend these first crucial 90 minutes every day to prepare for that opportunity.

It has been scientifically proven that in the morning, after a good night's sleep, we are more focused and energised than any other time of day or night. So if you are struggling to get something done, make it the first thing you do every day. The results will surprise you!

Now that you have learned how to make your universe favourable and keep it that way, let's move on to the third and final part of this book, where we discuss why some people don't get what they desire from the universe, despite doing everything right.

Part III

Whenever I have shared the concept of a favourable universe and its related challenges with my friends, they have always come back with one common question, which may have crossed your mind too at some point. The question is: I've done everything in my power to make my universe favourable. Then why am I still not getting what I asked for?

The answer to that is actually quite simple: there is still a little bit of fine-tuning left to do before you can get what you desire. Let's see how.

Chapter 8

Why are you still not getting what you asked for?

Gautam, a friend of mine and a soon-to-be lawyer, said, 'I think I have a favourable universe now. I'm facing the challenges we discussed and I'm working on them, but I still feel I'm far, far away from where I want to be. I don't think there's any person or thing or addiction stopping me. Maybe I'm not that well prepared, but still I don't see any clear signs or opportunities that can take me to the next step. I've done everything right, but it feels like I've come to a standstill.'

I realised it was time to introduce my friend to '**the missing element in the universe**'.

Nothing is perfect in life. No matter how favourable you think your universe is, it will never be perfect. It can be perfect only under one condition – when you are completely happy and satisfied with where you are in life and you have no zeal left in you to grow.

Even if you have a favourable universe, there will always be people, skills or opportunities that you will find missing in your life – elements that could help you get to the next step, provided you have worked out everything else. Ever heard someone saying, 'I wish I had some connection in that place; then my work would have been done much faster and easier'?

Let's take an *example*. If you want to be an influencer in your field today, there is one mandatory skill you need to possess – how to use social media. It doesn't matter if you learn it on your own or from an expert, but this skill is crucial to your success. At the moment this skill is missing from your life, and if you want it bad enough, you will have to work on acquiring it.

Similarly, if you observe deeply, you will find something or someone missing in your universe. Your job is to find those missing elements. As you keep finding them, you will see your life getting better and you will move one step closer to your goal.

Gaining some resources or skills takes more time than others, but if you are dedicated and serious, they will come your way sooner or later, because, as you know by now, you will get what you seek from the universe (the law of attraction).

The universe will itself help you find these missing elements by sending you signals in different ways.

Chapter 9

Signals from your universe

By now we are clear that the universe has all the answers we are looking for. It has mysterious ways of teaching us what we need to know, by sending us signals every now and then.[5] These signals guide us to what we truly want to achieve.

However, these signals are not always easy to catch. Sometimes they may come to you and you won't even know, **because they will be disguised as challenges**. For example, you may have to go through a devastating breakup to get the love of your life. You may lose someone you are completely dependent on just so that you can learn to count on your own self.

You will need to look beyond the suffering to recognise these signals.

Having said that, there are *three prominent and repetitive signals* the universe sends us to show us where we are meant to be and what we need to do to get there.

---

[5] https://www.youtube.com/watch?v=2JMwsnYDjsQ&t=442s

If you pay close attention to these signals, you can create the life of your dreams.

The lightning of joy

I don't want you to confuse joy with happiness, because joy is a *more permanent state* than happiness. Most of the times, happiness is tied to some achievement, outcome or other external force, but **joy is internal**. Joy is the continuous state of being happy that comes from just doing your best, detaching yourself from the results.

Joy is the ultimate tracking system to know that you are doing what you are meant to be doing. When you are living the life you want, you will be in a perpetual state of joy. If you are constantly frustrated or tired, it's a sign that you are not doing what you should be doing and you know that. Now your job is to look for that joy.

You owe it to yourself to do things that will make you joyful. And remember, today **it is possible to monetise work that brings you joy**. We live in an era where everything can be monetised. Once you give it your all, I am sure you will find a way, so please stop ignoring the signal of joy from the universe.

(The problem is there are certain fears that stop us from doing what we have always wanted to do. Later in the book I share how to eliminate those fears.)

Signals from your body

Have you ever felt pain in your body without being tired or for no other apparent reason? This pain is a sign of something the universe is trying to tell you.

The whole purpose of pain is to alert our body and mind that something is not right. And it's not necessary that we will feel pain only if we get injured or tired. There is scientific evidence that pain can be a physical manifestation of mental stress that is killing us inside, or some unhealed emotional wound. This physical pain can range from stomach ulcers to one of the most agonising pains ever endured by humankind, angina pectoris.

The problem is that we rarely pay attention to pain. We either ignore it or suppress it by calling it different names like tiredness, stiffness or fatigue. We try to make it go away with temporary solutions like medicines, alcohol, smoking or drugs. But instead of healing, we get addicted to these 'remedies', which only worsens our physical and mental health.

If you frequently experience pain of any kind, pay attention to it. Listen to what your body is trying to tell you, because it could be the universe trying to get you to listen.

By paying attention to this pain rather than ignoring it, you will heal the trauma that may be stopping you from achieving your dreams.

Signals from your brain

Have you ever had this experience where a song won't stop playing in your head? Happens often, right? Now if you have trained your mind to receive messages from the universe, you will notice that the lyrics of the song are the exact message that you wanted to hear at that point in time. Maybe, those lyrics are pointing to a situation you are in currently or will be sometime soon.

Or, there may be a recurring dream haunting or troubling you for a while. This dream could be signalling at something that is about to happen. I had such an experience recently that I would like to share for your better understanding.

Last year I had a very important meeting and I knew that a positive response from this meeting could be a game changer for me. For three nights in a row before the meeting I kept having the same dream: I am in my school, petrified about a class test that is about to happen. I haven't prepared for it, so I know I'm going to flunk.

Each night I woke up in a sweat after a hard slap from my teacher for failing the test.

My meeting didn't go well. I understood what went wrong, but it was too late by then. I had already lost my chance. Looking back, I was convinced that the dream was a signal from the universe. It was trying to tell me that I was not prepared for the meeting and needed to do more work to crack it. If I had understood the message the universe was trying to give me, I may have done things differently.

The universe has mysterious ways to teach us what we need to learn. So be conscious always and try to relate these signs with what's going on in your personal and professional life. If you are able to make the connection, you will be surprised with what you discover!

Now that you are aware of the existence of these signals, you can ask the universe for guidance and be more conscious of any such signals coming to you.

Chapter 10

Questions we ask the universe (putting an end to existential crisis)

In this last section of the book, I will be answering the most frequent and favourite questions we ask the universe. No matter where you live in the world or what you do, some or all of these questions must have crossed your mind. And I will not be surprised if you are still looking for answers, because only a while back I was too.

I have researched these questions extensively and tried to summarise the answers in the most understandable, relatable and simplest way possible. I hope these answers will bring light to your life as they have brought to mine. I request you to read these answers with an open mind, and even if some of them challenge your existing beliefs, just give them a try and see what happens.

Existential crisis

Humans are the only species that face existential crisis. So if you are human and alive, chances are you must have faced existential crisis at some point in your life.

To explain simply, existential crisis are moments when you ask or search for meaning of the big questions: **What is the purpose or meaning of my life? What exactly is happiness? How can I be happy?**

What is troubling is that some of us who don't get satisfactory answers to these questions get frustrated and may even go into depression. So the next time you or a loved one faces existential crisis, I urge you to open this part of the book and read it aloud to them. I have tried to answer the most frequent questions we ask of the universe when existential crisis strikes. If you can't find your question or your answer here, you can write to me personally.

What is the purpose of my life?

I have heard this question often and read about it extensively. I found that most self-help content is centred around this question, so why not simplify it.

I think the word *purpose* sells well because it has always been linked to achieving greatness or doing something that has never been done before. It is so overhyped that today everyone is frantically looking for their purpose and everyone wants to be great, but the irony is that if everyone is great, then, in a way, everyone is ordinary. (Read it once more. Think about it.)

I agree that it's nice to hear someone say, 'I have found my purpose in life.' The self-help videos and articles have impacted us so much that the moment we hear that someone has found their purpose, we declare them superior to us. They become someone who will have everything they want in life (even if they may not even know what they are doing). I am also guilty of thinking this way at one point in my life and allowing it to confuse and even depress me.

Then, I started looking for my own answer to this question – an answer that was simple to understand and did not necessarily need to be fancy or acceptable to all. I was looking for the meaning of my life (if there was any), so I tried to get to the root of the question.

Soon, one thing became crystal clear: **No one, no matter how smart, successful or rich they are, can tell me what my purpose is in life.**

Why, then, do I bother listening to anyone? Why do I pay so much attention to people's opinion of me, my life and my decisions?

I realised that I wanted a definition of *purpose* with which I could resonate. I tried hard and was able to identify something that made it all clear. Let me explain how.

Every task or activity requires three things from us: time, energy and attention. We cannot do anything efficiently or effectively in the absence of any of these three elements. Even the simplest of things consume our time and energy and attention, even though we may not be really focused on that task.

Then there are activities that make us lose track of time. This doesn't mean that time has stopped or slowed down – it's just that we get into a zone where we don't care about time anymore. We do these activities effortlessly and with complete focus. If there is any such activity in your life, then, my friend, you are blessed.

Now, I need you to pause and do an exercise.

Step 1: Take a pen and paper and write down a minimum of five activities that make you lose track of time. It could be anything: from something as routine as driving to work or cleaning up your room to spending time with a grandparent or mentoring someone or travelling on your own. List at least five such activities, and more if you can.

Step 2: Now rank these activities from most enjoyable (Rank 1) to least enjoyable (Rank 5).

Step 3: Now, from the top three activities, select one activity that you tend to do well – that is, where you think your performance is usually above average. Don't worry if it's something as simple as starting a conversation with someone – it takes a lot to do that.

Step 4: Next, pair your highest ranked activity (one that makes you happiest) with the activity selected in Step 3 (one that you do better than anything). This is your most favourable combination.

Step 5: Now, start thinking what you can do with this combination. Can you build a business out of it or take up a job in that field? Can you turn it into a second career or a weekend gig?

Let's say the activity that makes you happiest is watching good movies and the activity that you do better than anything is making videos on your phone. Why not combine the two and review films on YouTube?

Let your thoughts flow. Brainstorm. We are living in times where **anything can be turned into a source of income**, no matter how rare or vague the activity may sound to conventional thinkers. People are making a living out of giving reactions to film trailers! So you know what I mean.

Congratulations! You have found your purpose.

It's difficult to change our perceptions instantly, so take your time to absorb what you just discovered about yourself; let it sink in. Read your list again and again. Once you have the clarity, anything will seem achievable. And please don't be surprised or think that I have fooled you. Just thank the universe for blessing you with the ability to think, introspect, analyse and take action.

A tried and tested tip: Don't bother sharing your idea with anyone unless you are absolutely sure that no one can change your mind. No one knows you better than you, so don't let anyone tell you that you can't do it just because they are saying you can't.

There's one more thing I would like to add here: **It is OK if the activity that interests you changes over time. It's normal!**

For instance, in our twenties most of us only want to make money, and we are ready to do anything for it – work overtime, miss our favourite activities, neglect our families and so on. But as we grow older, we realise that money is not what we need to feel happy or fulfilled. Money doesn't interest us as much anymore.

Does this mean you are lost or that your purpose has changed? No. It simply means that you are no more as interested in something as you were a few years ago – and it's perfectly normal. In fact, it's great, because you were able to realise this and rediscover your purpose.

Once you have found your purpose, no matter where you are in life, how old you are or how much money you make, go after it. Do anything and everything it takes to achieve it. Because **life's ROI is not money but to be able to spend it your way.**

Lastly, no matter what your purpose, let it be something that serves humanity in some way and helps you leave the world a better place than it was when you arrived. The good thing is that you can do this in your own small way regardless of your circumstances.

Should we believe in luck or in hard work?

I have heard this question so often. In fact, I have been asked this quite a few times, and, honestly, I have not been able to answer it until recently.

I have this habit of posing questions to everyone I meet (especially those questions for which I don't have an answer myself). So I began asking everyone: Should we believe in luck or in hard work?

Some said we can't have anything we desire unless it's written in our destiny. Some said we can create whatever we want as our destiny is in our own hands. Both these answers seemed incomplete to me.

If destiny is predefined, then why do we hustle day and night? And what if we find that, no matter how hard we try, we can't have some things in life?

If we create our own destiny, then why don't some of us even have enough food to eat? I think everyone must have the right to at least create this much of destiny, so that no one will starve to death.

In my search for the right answer, I met one of my teachers and asked him the same question.

He said he would tell me the answer, but I would have to make *two promises*. 'First, you will not ask anyone this question ever again,' he said, 'and second, you will not question why I asked you to make the first promise. I made these same promises to my guru when I asked him this question.'

I was surprised and confused, yet I did not mind making those promises. Knowing my teacher, I was sure he had a rock-solid answer to this. And if I received a satisfactory reply, why would I need to ask the question ever again? I would then be more interested in sharing that knowledge with others.

I agreed and he continued, 'What I'm going to tell you is a mix of *psychology and spirituality*. I hope you will understand it and realise it sooner or later. Right or wrong, I found this to be the only satisfactory answer to live by. Here it goes:

Imagine a cow tethered to a peg. It can only graze as far as the length of rope tied to its neck. So, the circumference made by the rope is your luck, and this luck is defined by *Sanchita Karma*. But to reach and have access to everything on the circumference, you will have to make effort, or you won't be able to get even what's already in store for you. This effort or doing is your *Prarabdha Karma*. That is why you should always be on your toes to do your best. Who knows, you might just break the rope and increase your circumference!

And even if you are not able to break the rope, you will at least get all that is meant for you and at the same time enhance your *Agami Karma*.'

There are three types of Karma:[6]

1. **Sanchita karma** is the karma of past life. It is the storehouse of all the *karm* we have done in our past lives.

2. **Prarabhda karma** is what we are doing in the present, in this lifetime, and its result.

3. **Agami karma** is the future karma that will result from our present actions.

---

6 https://www.doyouyoga.com/the-3-types-of-karma-explained/

As we attempt to balance our past karmas, we unavoidably create new karmas, which we may or may not be able to resolve in our present lives. If we don't resolve them now, they will go into the storehouse, to be resolved in a future life.

In summary, my teacher helped me understand that it is karma, or work, that we should be focused on. **We can change our destiny with our actions, if we so desire.**

I understand that not everyone reading this book may believe in karma. As I want this book to reach as many people as it can and resonate with as many beliefs as it can, I have a different solution for those who don't believe in the concept of karma.

I want to give you a purely psychological explanation of believing in hard work over luck, because the moment you realise that hard work is superior to luck, or that there is no such thing as luck at all, you will start appreciating everyone who has achieved something in their life. Instead of being jealous of them, you will be inspired by them, because now you know that they are there because they worked for it.

***

Let's talk about feelings. to better understand the connection between luck and hard work.

First and foremost, let me make it clear that feelings are internal – that is, **how you feel in a situation does**

not depend on the situation but on what you think of that situation.

Let me share an example. Remember the time from your childhood when your best friend was punished for a mischief you did together? You may have felt some relief, but how did your friend feel?

Or, say, you suddenly bumped into your ex and they looked better than ever. You had a feeling of regret and they might have had a feeling of pride or arrogance.

The point I am trying to make here is that, if feelings were dependent on our external environment, everyone will have the same feeling in a particular event. Your ex and you, or you and your friend at school, would have felt the same. What changes the two feelings is what is happening inside us. That's why a person cheating another person has no idea what's going on inside the person being cheated.

Once we understand that feelings are internal, it becomes easier for us to control them, because now our feelings are independent of what's happening outside. Let's start with a small example and see if you can control your feelings.

It is a universal phenomenon that those who know driving think that they are one of the best drivers in the world (it's good in a way, to be confident – but not overconfident – of your driving skills. It helps avoid accidents). But when such people are out driving, they get upset when they see others drive recklessly.

The next time you are on the road, try not to get angry about someone else's driving. Because it only creates disturbance within you and changes nothing for that person. Remind yourself: This situation and my state of mind have no connection. I decide my state of mind – no one else has the power to do it.

Starting with such small, everyday incidents, try to control your inner feelings in bigger situations and events, like heartbreak. I am not saying that you should become heartless, but try and avoid reactions like anger and anxiety. These negative feelings and emotions only harm you and others around you, with no productive outcome for anyone. In sum, you and only you should have the power of how you feel.

So how does this relate to the question of luck versus hard work. It's simple. When you learn that feelings are internal, you gain the power to change them. So the next time you feel that you are not good enough or someone else is more successful, you can change those feelings. You can tell yourself that your circumstances are not created by luck but by your own actions – and you can change those circumstances with hard work.

The power of choice

The presence of Prarabdha Karma brings me to another point: that we always have a choice. Indeed, there are things beyond our control and we don't have a choice but to accept them (for example, we didn't get to choose our parents, the city or country where we were born, our physical appearance, our religion or our socio-economic class). Similarly, we don't get to choose our Death (unless someone takes the unfortunate decision of taking their own life).

But whatever happens in between our birth (or the time when we come to our senses) and death is our choice. Whatever is written in our destiny according to the Sanchita Karma can be achieved (or not) depending on the choices we make in the present. For instance, it may be in your destiny to win a million dollars in a lottery, but whether you spend this million on partying and poker or invest it and multiply it is entirely up to you. I don't know whether a lion has the choice to skip its lunch or the choice to be vegetarian or non-vegetarian; or, whether a frog gets to choose its menu of dinner or breakfast; or if a kitten spends hours in getting ready for a party. **But we humans do have a choice.**

From deciding what to wear to what impact we are leaving on society, our life is based on the choices we make. We may not make some choices consciously, but each choice makes a difference. Every decision, whether eating something or not, meeting someone or not, doing something or even not doing anything, has a different outcome. And these outcomes shape our personality, our present and our future. Whether we realise it or not, we are always choosing, from the moment we wake up to the moment we fall asleep.

Of course, some choices are easier than others. Some have a temporary effect (whether or not to have alcohol today), while some cling to us for a lifetime (choosing a life partner or a career). Choice is what makes us who we are or who we are going to be.

Once we realise that we always have a choice, life would be much easier. Because then we would start taking accountability of all our decisions, big and small, conscious or subconscious. Then, instead of blaming your luck for losing a million in poker, you would blame yourself for betting it all in the first place. Instead of blaming your lifestyle for excessive smoking or drinking, you would blame yourself for not being smart enough to know that they are bad for your health.

No matter who tells you what, in the end it is your choice to believe or act upon it – or not. People around you can only manipulate your decision making (which is why a favourable universe is necessary), but the final decision lies in your hands. If you commit a blunder due to a choice made under someone's influence, there would not be anyone else to blame but you.

The 90/10 principle

The power of choice reminds me of a principle by the world-famous author Stephen Covey. This principle is called the **90/10 principle**.[7]

This principle alone can completely transform your life. It states that only 10% of our life is made up of

---

7   https://www.knowfacts.info/2020/02/the-simple-principle-of-9010-that-affects-your-whole-life.html?m=1&utm_source=quora&utm_medium=referra

what happens to us – the rest 90% is decided by how we react to what happens to us. And how we react is our choice.

Let me illustrate this with a simple example. Suppose you are at the breakfast table with your family and your daughter (or sibling) accidently spills coffee on you. You scream at her, and then at your family for keeping the cup too close to the edge. You run to your room to change and come back to find that the child is still at the table, crying, and has missed her school bus. Now you have to drop her to school while you are already running late. On the entire way, you curse the traffic, which only worsens your mood and upsets the child even more.

These mood spoilers keep coming on loop the entire day, and you can't wait for the day to end. On top of it, when you are back home, you can sense that your family is still upset about the incident.

Now, stop for a while and think – was it the spilling of coffee that ruined the day? Probably not. It was your reaction to it. If you would have simply asked the child to be careful the next time, she would have reached school on time, in her school bus. You would have reached work on time, and everyone would have had a smooth day. Two entirely different scenarios that start the same but change along the way, based purely on your reaction aka choice.

Of course you can blame others for this too, but has it ever helped?

When you start taking responsibility for every choice you make, it makes you feel empowered. You free yourself from blaming others for your bad choices, and, simultaneously, you become aware that whatever you have achieved so far is only because of your own actions. Now you will be more careful in making choices – you have learned that you can become whatever you want provided you make the right choices needed to get there.

What is happiness (or how to be happy)?

Happiness is the most desired feeling. I believe it is also the most overrated. If feelings are internal, then why do we bind our happiness to things, people and situations all the time?

Why is it so difficult for us to understand that the more our happiness depends on external factors, the more hurt we will be? Why is there a need at all to ask how to be happy?

Yet, this is one of the most asked questions in the world. There are millions of videos with billions of views explaining how to be happy, which makes me wonder: Are so many of us really so deprived of happiness, as if it's buried somewhere and can't be accessed by the average human, that we need to go to life mentors or self-help coaches to find it?

In fact, we have asked this question so much that we have forgotten the real meaning of happiness. The truth is that **happiness is nowhere else but here.**

Most of us have a goal mindset – we set up a goal and we are happy only when we achieve it. If your happiness depends on achieving something, chances are you will always be looking for happiness. There will always be something to chase, and hence your pursuit will never be complete. As a result, you will never be completely happy.

We have always tied our happiness to something we are yet to own or some event that is yet to happen. We have always postponed our happiness to the future, whereas real happiness exists in the present. Yet, we fail to see it.

To be truly happy, we have to shift the goal mindset to a growth mindset, which states that happiness is in growing. We are growing every day. Whether we pass or fail, whether we achieve a goal or not, we always learn something, and this learning helps us grow. The growth mindset helps us grow exponentially and makes us understand that happiness is in the moment, in the present. Happiness is to feel alive, to be thankful for whatever we have.

Now, I need you to close your eyes and remember the last time you were the happiest. Were you thinking of your future at that time? Were you worried about how you will never be that happy again? If we keep dwelling on future happiness, it is certain that we will never be happy, because, as they say, **tomorrow never comes**.

Each one of us has played some sport or practised some form of art. When doing any such activity, we have to give our 100 percent, or we end up losing (or creating bad art). In the same way, if you look for happiness in a place other than the present, you will end up losing the real essence of happiness.

Seeking happiness elsewhere hurts you in two ways: You lose the happiness of the present moment, because you are imagining a situation that is yet to happen (or has already happened). Second, because you can't be in that imagined moment, you feel even worse about your current situation.

If you want to experience true happiness, focus on your present.

What is success?

Before discussing the true meaning of success, I want to clear some myths around success, many of which have been prevalent in our society for decades now. Worryingly, many of these have been accepted as facts that people now follow blindly, no questions asked.

Myth: success is a general term

Fact: We have learned that every individual is unique and has a different purpose in life. I want to ask you a question here. *If everyone is different, then how can we generalise success?*

But we as a society have a very *narrow* definition of success. If you want to be called successful, you must have abundance of money, fame, power, and so on. This is a grossly incorrect definition of success. Just as your goals are different from mine, so will be your measures of success.

It is wrong to **generalise** success. It's only because of this generalisation that so many people are in a constant pressure 'to succeed'. We all know very well how this affects people's mental health, sometimes to the point of suicide. **This needs to stop.**

I have heard numerous speeches, seen dozens of videos and read a lot of success-related content; unfortunately, most of them propagate this generalised notion of success, which, I believe, is the most widespread and common myths of them all.

Success is not about your bank balance or the number of your Instagram followers. We are all different, so our success cannot come from the same thing, nor can it be compared. How can we judge success by just one or two common measures like money or fame?

We are all living different lives, with different mindsets, in different circumstances, and our success will vary accordingly. For example, a teacher may not be rich, but if they are able to help their students to be great at a subject, that's success.

Similarly, a successful NGO (non-government organisation) is not one that is able to accumulate stacks of cash, but one that has really made a difference in society. A great problem-solving business may not be the richest business, but that doesn't mean it's not successful.

Google Maps, for example, is a huge problem-solver and timesaver, but it's not the most revenue-generating business for Google.

So I urge you to stop generalising success. And remember, **you need not justify your success to anyone on any particular parameter.**

If you do want to have a general definition of success, create your own with some common ingredients that everyone needs to succeed in any type of work. I will reveal these ingredients right after this section because, in order to understand and apply them in your success mix, you need to first let go of these myths.

Myth: it's easy once you get there

Fact: Let us be very clear: it's never easy. Let's remove this notion from our minds that it's going to be a smooth ride once you have reached your goal.

Someone rightly said, what comes easy won't last, and what lasts won't come easy. When we are striving to achieve something worthy, all the hard work and time that we put in are actually preparing us for the future. We are being conditioned to deal with the pressure and responsibility that will come once we are at the peak. Put simply, the hard work that you are doing now is getting you ready for all the long days and sleepless nights that lie ahead.

So if you think that it will get easy once you are successful, you may be in for a surprise.

Myth: they got lucky

Fact: Easier said than done, right? People often say that someone was lucky to get the chance they got. They were lucky to be there at that moment. They got lucky that things turned out in their favour.

Yes, sometimes people get lucky, and there is nothing wrong with that. But maybe they got lucky because they worked hard to reach the place where luck would turn in their favour. To quote the acclaimed golfer Gary Player, 'The harder you work, the luckier you get.'

This reminds me of an incident where a guy who had multiple food outlets in a city had to close eighty percent of his outlets due to a change in government policies. One day, he went to a conference to hear a leading entrepreneur share his lessons from failure. In the Q&A session, my friend asked the speaker: 'I've recently been failed by the government. What would you do if you were at my place?'

He didn't get a satisfactory answer, but later someone walked up to him and said, 'Don't worry that you can't have more outlets in your city. You have the entire country to explore and then the entire world, and I'm ready to help you. I will invest in your business.' The collaboration took off and eventually turned out to be a profitable investment for both.

Now, **would you call my friend lucky, or would you say he worked hard to be in that place?** If your answer is that he worked for it, then you better start working.

If the answer is that he was lucky, then, too, you better start working hard, because not everyone in this world is lucky.

In sum, whenever we call someone lucky, we fail to see all the work they did to get there.

You need to be crystal-clear on these myths, because these are sometimes used as excuses by people who aren't successful. **It's YOU who wants success, so it's you has to do the work.**

Now let us take a step forward and understand what success actually is.

An ideal success mix

A person's success depends on their perspective of success, and on what they want to achieve in life. **However, every definition of success has some common ingredients. These are important elements for success, just like salt is an important and common ingredient in every dish** (even some desserts have salt in them). Every person's success turns out to be different based on how these ingredients are combined.

There are three main ingredients for success. Each one of them is so powerful that if any one of them goes missing at any point, you can again turn unsuccessful, not to society but to yourself, because success, my friend, is a very personal thing.

Excitement: Are you someone who spends their days slogging, just to feel exhausted and unfulfilled at the end of the day?

Are you someone who keeps busy just to avoid asking yourself that one question: Am I really enjoying what I am doing? Does coming to work daily excite you, or do you show up just because you need to (because otherwise you would starve to death)?

Work, my friend, takes most of our time and energy. We spend more time at work than we do with our family or friends. If you are not even remotely excited in those working hours, then you are wasting your life. I may sound harsh, but that's the truth.

Work has a huge impact on our lives as a whole. It shapes our personality and our life. A successful person lives an active lifestyle whereas an unsuccessful (or soon-to-be-unsuccessful) person lives a passive lifestyle. Let me explain the difference between the two, so that you can judge for yourself which category you belong to.

Active Lifestyle vs Passive Lifestyle

Sometimes, the most complicated questions have the simplest answers. If you want to know how to achieve success in your life, the answer lies in changing your lifestyle.

Have you ever wondered why, despite everyone having twenty-four hours a day, some of us accomplish so much more than others? Lifestyle is the answer. It is the most significant and life-changing difference between those who achieve their dreams and those who don't, though it may not seem that way to most of us. I myself have been a victim of this for an entire year, and this was when I was well aware that I was trapped in a passive lifestyle. Imagine how tough it would be for someone who is not even aware that their lifestyle is holding them back.

Interestingly, this vicious circle starts with a day and turns into a routine before you know.

The difference between an active and a passive lifestyle is simple: **Do you run your day or does it run you?** Does your day start even before you are out of bed?

If you have several missed calls from work even before you wake up, or if most people are having lunch by the time you are thinking of what to have for breakfast, welcome to the passive lifestyle. Of course there are exceptions, and there are days when this behaviour is acceptable, but if this is happening to you even when you don't want it to, you are stuck in a passive lifestyle.

Fortunately, you can change this. Instead of being a victim of your day, grab it by the neck and put it to use as you want. If you use just enough days as per your wish, you will by default create an active lifestyle – and hence a great life.

Now coming to the second ingredient of the ideal success mix.

Giving: Most of us are convinced that happiness or success lies in possession. But this is not true. Real success is much beyond owning things. If you look at successful entrepreneurs, or even successful people in general, you will find that most have given back to society or created something for the greater good. Of course, every business must make money, but an honest desire to help others through your work will ensure that your business is recognised and valued by society.

Ever thought where the likes of TATA or Microsoft would be if they had stopped just when they achieved enough wealth for their personal needs? Their efforts to serve the society not only helped those in need, it also helped these businesses earn a special place in our hearts and minds.

Let me explain how giving has an impact on our minds and therefore our lives.

What you give returns to you manifold. If you give something to someone – it could be anything: your knowledge or expertise, a product or service, or even good advice – you will have a sense of satisfaction. When you help those who are worse off than you, it will motivate you to help as many people as you can. You will start appreciating your life and yourself.

At some point, you may have thought (or may have been told) that you are good for nothing, or that you suck as a person, but there is no truth in this. Giving will help you realise this. It will boost your self-respect, because when you make someone smile, you get the feeling that you are creating a better world around you. So look for opportunities where you could be of service to someone. You will grow as a person every time you do that – which brings me to the next point.

Growing: Success is not real if the process did not help you grow as an individual. In fact, if success does not bring any positive change in you (i.e., if you remain the same as you were when you were not successful), your success will not last. Success should help you grow, and the only way to grow is by failing. Yes, you read that right. The only way we grow is by failure.

Every failure takes us one step further, because with every trial we eliminate the methods that are not working. Frank Wilczek, the 2004 Nobel Prize co-winner in Physics, once said, **'If you don't make mistakes, you are not working on hard enough problems. And that's a big mistake.'**

You can be very rich and have a very great social life, but you can't be fully content if you have nothing left to look forward to, or if you think you have nothing left to achieve. That's the reason why we see CEOs and co-founders of such big companies as Instagram and Flipkart quitting when they realise they have reached the end of the road in terms of individual growth. They know they can't grow anymore by being in the same environment or company, so they move on in search of new adventures.

How to be successful?

Now that you are aware of the common ingredients of success, you will find it easier to understand how you can be successful.

You may have come across the phrase 'how to be successful' a million times – you may even have searched for it online. Some of the answers may have helped you, yet others may have been disappointing because you didn't feel they applied to your field or your specific concern.

There is one question that everyone has asked at some point: How are some people in the world so successful while others struggle to even earn a living? I was also disturbed by this same question. In trying to find an answer, I started to follow each and every influencer I could think of – entrepreneurs, artists, health coaches, anyone who has made it big. Then I tried to find some similarity between them, and, believe me, it was not as difficult as I thought it would be. I learned that all of them followed some basic principles or habits in life, which, in spite of being simple, are not easy to follow. I have tried my best to relate those principles with the theme of this book.

I will give you **three habits and one principle** that will help you be successful, no matter which industry or which part of the world you are in, or what phase of life. These tools will work regardless of the type of goals you have or the career you have chosen. These habits are extracted from the universe and hence, they are universal.

Let's start with the Principle.

Visualisation

To succeed, you need to have this principle, or rather power, of visualising exactly what you are aiming for. The reason is simple: we can't achieve what we can't think of, and if we can't think of something, how would we visualise it? Visualisation is one step ahead of thinking. Once your thoughts are clear and precise, you will be able to visualise your goal.

Most of us have an idea of what we want to do or where we want to be, but the problem is that we don't fully believe in it. We are scared of dreaming big, and because of this we often settle for much less than we deserve. The moment we have complete belief in our goal, we will be able to visualise it exactly. And the more vivid our visualisation, the more motivated we will feel to take action and achieve what we have visualised.

For example, if money is what you are asking for, visualise how you would live when you have that money. How would you dress? What would your surroundings be like? Go a step ahead and think of how you would feel having all that money.

To master the art of visualisation, you need to be aware of one trick or formula:

Filtering out

Today is the era of options. From what to eat, what to wear, what to do and where to go – we have too many options to choose from. Choice is important, but too much choice distracts us from our goals. It consumes our energy and our time. In fact, we end up draining so much of our energy in the process that by the time we have to make a decision, we are too tired. As a result, we often end up choosing the wrong option and regret it later.

This might not have happened if we didn't have so much choice in the first place.

The perception of 'more is good' has become so widespread that it's suffocating us now. Thankfully, we have the universe to our rescue. Things might have changed, the style of doing business may have changed, but one thing is constant and is still appreciated is what the universe taught us millions of years ago – that **greatness lies in simplicity**.

Even today, when you look at the world's most successful brands (think Apple or Google), they have always worked around the idea of simplicity – and their tremendous success validates this ideology.

So filter out all the clutter, focus on one thing and start visualising it. Visualise it repeatedly, and soon you will find yourself consciously or subconsciously working in that direction.

Next up, I share the three common habits or traits you will need to be successful.

Treat everyone equally

This simply means that you must treat every single individual in your universe as equals. By that I don't mean being rude or abusive with everyone, because that's also treating people equally. What I mean is to practise the kind of equality with which the universe treats us.

No matter how rich or poor you are, how young or old, you get the same oxygen from plants as everyone else.

The wind hits each and every one equally. The rain pours on everyone. So, by treating everyone equally I mean giving respect to everyone irrespective of their position in your life or in society. If you see someone being ill-treated, always be ready to help them in whatever way you can.

Be consistent

Some days the sun's rays are warm enough to tan the body; some days they are good enough to be enjoyed; and on others they simply hide behind the clouds. But one thing is sure: the sun shows up daily – it is consistent.

The same happens with us in life. Some days we are fully charged and motivated to get out and rule the world. Some days we feel good enough to serve the world, and then there are days when we don't even want to get out of bed.

The message I want to convey here is this: If you are constant enough (i.e., if you are working even on your bad days), that will make all the difference. That is what differentiates an average person from the successful person, because it's easier to make excuses than to actually go out there and work.

Think of the greater good

The universe is always giving. Trees give us shade. Plants give us food. Flowers give us fragrance. Nature gives us so much without expecting anything in return. We don't have to pay or do anything special to get all of this.

Everything is abundant and absolutely free, and that's how the human world should be. Instead of letting each other down, we should help each other grow.

Most people confuse success with possession. They believe success is achieving things, and that too materialistic things. We have created a stereotype that having more money, more cars, more houses is what makes one successful. But if we go by this theory, we can never be successful, simply because there will always be someone having more cars or more money. (When it came to wealth, even Bill Gates was beaten by the Amazon founder Jeff Bezos!) Moreover, this greed of having more never lets one feel contented. What use is success if it doesn't bring peace and satisfaction?

I believe that real success is in what the universe teaches us – to give. As beings of the universe, we all have something unique; in other words, we all have something in excess over others. All we have to do is find that something and share it with the world. It could be anything: a skill, a talent, a trait.

For those who haven't found this something yet or believe that they don't have any unique or special quality, don't worry. You can develop it, as I developed the habit of reading and writing before writing this book.

Believe me, the ecstasy you will feel after giving that something to the world is incomparable. You can share your uniqueness with the world through teaching, consulting, mentoring or even helping. If you can monetise this sharing of knowledge, that's icing on the cake, because then you are getting both joy and money.

I hope more and more people can find success by this method.

How to stop being lazy and get going?

Laziness is a word that should be deleted from the dictionary of life.

Before we discuss this further, let's first understand that laziness is different from procrastination (though the reason behind both is often the same). Procrastination means avoiding the task at hand by doing unimportant tasks, while laziness is total inaction or wanting to do nothing at all.

Often, procrastination will eventually turn into laziness. There is indeed no harm in being lazy for a day or two or when on a vacation, but being in a lazy state for long periods of time is definitely something you want to look into.

Here I am sharing a solution that will help you get rid of both procrastination and laziness. I would rather call it a trick, and if used efficiently, this trick will help you do even the hardest tasks with ease. I have recently started using this and found amazing results instantly. To better understand this, you will first have to understand the functioning of the pleasure hormone, Dopamine. Dopamine is a double-edged sword, so understanding it is necessary to use it for your benefit.[8]

---

8   https://www.youtube.com/watch?v=QVf36rZQyCY&t=4s

No matter whatever we do, a certain amount of dopamine gets released in your brain. Now, obviously, different activities cause different amounts of dopamine release, which is why we like some activities more than others. The problems starts when our brain becomes habitual of this dopamine rush (a sudden release of dopamine in more quantity than usual). It gets worse when we figure out which activities cause this rush, because then we would want to do more of those activities. On an average, a person does more activities that result in dopamine rush than those that don't.

Interestingly, activities that have a random outcome (or no fixed outcome) release more dopamine than those with a fixed outcome. For example, activities like gaming, surfing the internet, watching random videos and gambling cause the brain to release more dopamine, and before we know it our brain becomes addicted to this rush. As a result we start avoiding focused activities with fixed end results – we find them boring. Examples of such activities are studying, making a business plan, exercising or doing household chores.

Let me give you a hypothetical example to help you understand this better. Think of a food you hate eating or don't like that much in general (for me it's black olives). Now imagine being stuck on an island with nothing solid to eat, no internet or other source of entertainment, and nowhere else to go except a nearby stall that only serves the food you hate. If it happened to me, I'm pretty sure I would eat all the olives I can.

Today our lives are flooded with dopamine rush, largely because social media is such an integral part of our lives. We have quick access to anything we want; everything is available online. Want to eat a pizza? Three to four clicks, and boom! It will be at your doorstep in less than thirty minutes. Want to play a game but have no friends to play with? No problem! Go online and you'll find thousands of people waiting for you to play with them. All this easy access to everything has affected our brains so much that now when we have to do anything that will not bring instant results our brain stops us from doing it.

The simple solution here is to have a fixed schedule, where you promise yourself not to use social media or do any kind of casual internet browsing for a fixed time, especially the morning hours. This will prevent you from getting a dopamine rush first thing in the morning. This way you will be able to keep a check on your brain and do things (or will at least try to do things) that you avoid or don't like doing in general.

A step ahead in neutralising your brain is to go on a **dopamine fast** to detox your brain of dopamine. Try every once in a while, preferably once a week, to be away from all your gadgets and all kinds of screens. Refrain from consuming any fast food or artificial flavours. And you will notice a drastic change in you. You will feel calmer and more willing to try and do new and different things.

And once you start something new, remember to keep your expectations low – don't expect to be a millionaire within one year of starting your business or to be a bestselling author after writing your *first book*. I am not asking you not to wish or aspire for success – just don't overburden yourself with unrealistic expectations. Start small. Think of what you are going to accomplish today and now. Give yourself the smallest possible tasks; for example, if you want to write a book, start by writing just 100 words a day. Don't think about the entire book; worry about the current chapter for now.

The problem with setting high expectations of yourself is that it stops you from doing anything at all.

Let's say you have been thinking of clearing your office clutter for a while now. You keep postponing it as you think you don't have the time. If you just lowered your expectation a little and started with cleaning the stationery drawer first, then the file cabinet, and so on, you will find your office free of clutter sooner than expected. If a task looks daunting, start small, and once you have built momentum, raise your target manifolds. Who knows, you might become a millionaire in just six months, or your first book could become an international bestseller. This way you can win over laziness or procrastination for sure.

Now that you have a sure-shot formula of kicking laziness out of your life, let me take you one step ahead.

Laziness can return if you don't have any motivation to keep doing what you are doing. This motivation will set you on a path where you will never stop to look back at your lazy days.

After much observation, I learned that motivation can be divided into certain levels or types. I call it the Motivational Pyramid. Read on to know which level of this pyramid you are at currently.

The motivation pyramid

I believe that our level of motivation directly impacts the actions we take, and the actions we take directly impact our motivation. There can be no action without motivation. And the opposite is also true: the more we work on something, the more motivated we feel about it.

I remember reading *The Subtle Art of Not Giving a Fuck* by Mark Manson, where he

introduces the **'Do Something' principle:** Action isn't just the effect of motivation; it's also the cause of it.

Manson explains that 'if you lack the motivation to make an important change in your life, do something, anything really, and then harness the reaction to that action as a way to begin motivating yourself.'[9]

The level of motivation keeps changing, based on our core values, our company and our life experiences. And all our actions are based on the level of motivation we feel inside us.

9 https://markmanson.net/how-to-get-motivated

I have divided people into three categories based on their levels of motivation. Most people, but not all, move up this hierarchy as they move ahead in life.

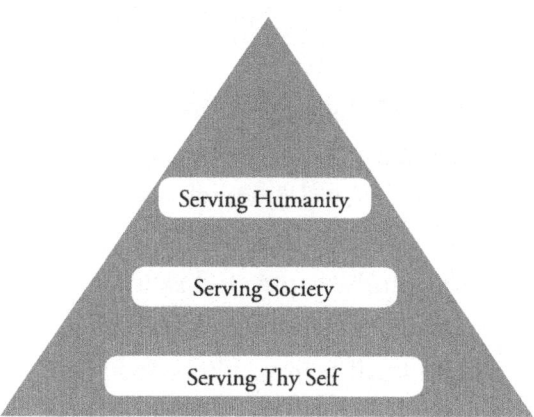

Level 1: These people are generally found doing jobs with decent pay that give them a sense of security. They are concerned with having a safe future while feeding themselves well in the present. These people are generally those whom our society terms as 'average'.

Level 2: These people have greater motivation and hence a broader perspective of life. Not only are they concerned about themselves and their families, but they also want to serve the society they live in or the clients they serve. Most of these individuals have upgraded from Level 1. Middle-class entrepreneurs and high-level executives are examples of such people.

Level 3: These individuals are few in numbers, but they have the most impact on humankind, because their main motive in life is to help people. Generally, they have crossed levels 1 and 2 of motivation. They are less selfish now as they have almost achieved all the materialistic things they once desired. They are forever ready to help others because they know the pain of helplessness – they have been there.

Not everyone will follow this hierarchy of motivation. Some people will be at Level 1 all their lives, while some will directly jump to Level 3 without ever being at levels 1 or 2. There is nothing wrong with being at any level of motivation. You can be happy and satisfied at any level. But if you want to move to the next level and don't know how, this pyramid will help you know why and what are you lacking and what steps you can take to reach the next level.

There is a more traditional explanation of laziness.

I would like to end this book with an incident that changed me forever.

I was home after my board exams and was feeling damn bored. All my friends had flown back to their hometowns, so I had no one to hang out with. Phone conversations also got boring after a while. I had been home two weeks and had done everything I could do to pass my time. I called my father one afternoon and told him I was feeling extremely bored. I asked him if he could come home or give me something to do that would keep me busy. He said he was busy that evening and asked me to wake up at six the next morning.

'I will teach you an exciting game,' he said, 'and once you know how to play it, you'll never be bored.'

I begged him to tell me the name of the game but he didn't. Anyhow, this created new levels of excitement in me. I couldn't stop wondering if there was really a game or my father was just fooling around with me. Also, why hadn't I discovered this game until now?

I couldn't sleep that night. A thousand thoughts went through my mind. I scoured the internet but found nothing. To my surprise, the next morning I woke up at five and that too without an alarm. It was after a long time that I woke without hitting snooze. I was both excited and nervous about what was about to happen. My father came to see me at about 5.45 a.m. and I was ready by then. All he said was, 'As expected.'

I smiled. He smiled back and said that he would see me at the main gate sharp at six. I wore a tracksuit because I knew he went for a run every morning, so just to match up. We started running as soon as I reached the gate. Then he started talking.

Dad: Why did you wake up so early today?

Me: Because you told me to.

Dad: But, as far as I remember, I've told you the same thing about a zillion times, but I haven't seen you wake up this early ever. It's all about the game, right?

Me: Partially, yes.

Dad: I am your dad. I know this is not a partial but a full yes. I've been through this, and no matter how shameful it is to admit, but today I confess that when I was your age, I was even lazier – until your grandfather taught me this game that I'm going to teach you today.

Me: Stop making it more dramatic and tell me, please.

Dad: Okay, but don't interrupt. And keep all questions to yourself, because I'm not going to answer them anyway. You will get all your answers if you keep patience in the beginning.

Me: Okay. Now shoot.

Dad: The game I'm about to tell you about is called the Game of Life. It's the only game where your competitor is no one else but you. The sooner you understand this game, the more sorted out your life will be. You are sent on this planet with a purpose and you have to find that. **Laziness, my son, is simply lack of purpose.**

I wanted to say something, but kept quiet.

Dad continued. 'According to me only two types of people can be lazy, or have the right to be lazy. Those who have nothing to look forward to or have no purpose in life, and those who believe they have achieved everything in life and are just waiting for death. Laziness is a trap that's easy to get into but very difficult to get out of. Laziness is not a phrase or a term – it's a lifestyle. Because, when you are lazy it starts to impact your whole life.'

I stopped to catch my breath. He wasn't finished.

'There are two kinds of people in this world,' he said, 'those who take charge of their lives and those who let their lives take charge of them. The latter ones are usually called **lazy**. They let their surroundings decide what's good for them or what they can achieve. Now you decide, son, what kind of person you are, or want to be. I am not warning you or pressurising you to do something right away, but at least you can start exploring. You can take a step forward by eliminating the things that you know you don't want to do at all.'

'But we can only do something if we have the motivation to do it,' I said.

'Motivation doesn't make us take action. In fact, it's quite the opposite. The more action or efforts you put into a thing or an idea, the more motivated and confident you will feel. There can be no motivation without any action. So stop being lazy and start doing some action. What that action would be, I leave that for you to decide,' he concluded.

I had questions, and I tried to ask some, but he said he wanted me to find the answers myself.

I still remember that day so vividly, me trying to soak in all that information. But I guess I was too young to understand it all at that point of time. Now, when I look back, it all makes sense.

I have learned much in these past few years. I have seen people who, in spite of having all the money and fame they could dream of, are not happy. So many successful people are never happy and content with themselves. On the other hand, I have seen the glow on faces of those who have dedicated themselves in the service of others without expecting anything in return.

I, too, have decided to live my life in service – service of humanity and all living beings – in whichever way I can. I don't to want to just live for myself, earn money and die.

I want to help people. I want everyone to know that, no matter what they do or where they are born, they can achieve anything. And I think I am a step closer to my mission by writing this book.

Thank you for reading.

A note from the author

Dear Reader,

I would like to start by thanking the Universe, and if you have read this book, you know I have all the reasons to do so.

I chose this particular topic because I noticed that everyone around me was facing the same problems that I mentioned in this book, but somehow, they were not ready to talk about it. Or, maybe, in this era of social media, people feel that sharing their vulnerabilities will make them look weak.

My aim with this book was to lend a hand. Now you have something or someone (me!) to go to. I wanted to come across as a friend rather than a mentor or a philosopher and in my own small way help my readers overcome things that bog them down, however tough they think their situation to be. I hope I have initiated that process by writing this book.

I would like to thank you once again for investing your time and money in this book. (No thanks to those who got it for free – just kidding!)

A Note from the Author

A note of thanks to my editor, Neetu Ralhan, for her time and patience in helping me complete this book. It's a joy to finally see two years of my hard work in print.

That's all from me.

If you like anything about this book, please tell your friends, family and colleagues about it.

If you are interested in what I do next, please follow me on social media. My Instagram username is @*vishaldhingra6*.

You can also write to me officially or unofficially at vishaldhingra95@gmail.com. Your suggestions are always welcome.

Again, thank you so much for reading – I'm excited to be connected with you and wish to bring more such books to you.

Adios…!!! Until we meet next.

Made in the USA
Coppell, TX
26 February 2021

Made in the USA
Coppell, TX
15 November 2025